Haaaa!

Ha!

THE FUNNIEST BOOK OF JOKES EVER

Hee!

LOL!

igloobooks

Published in 2016
by Igloo Books Ltd
Cottage Farm
Sywell
NN6 0BJ
www.igloobooks.com

All images supplied courtesy of Thinkstock, Getty Images.

GUA006 0616
4 6 8 10 9 7 5 3
ISBN 978-1-78343-122-9

Printed and manufactured in China

THE FUNNIEST BOOK OF JOKES EVER

HAHA

HILARIOUS CONTENTS

LOL!

SILLY JOKES AND GROSS JOKES

Haaaa!

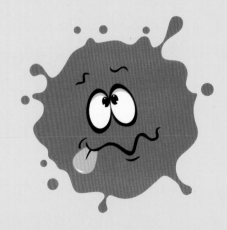

CAN YOU SMELL THAT?

Smelly jokes are great gross jokes.
Everybody loves a good smelly joke.
So come on and take a good sniff.
There's something really
disgusting in the air.

What did one
smelly sock say to the
other smelly sock?

"Are you stinking what
I'm stinking?"

What's big
and grey and stinks?

A smellyphant.

What's icky, yellow and
smells like bananas?

Monkey vomit.

What do you call a fairy who hasn't taken a bath?

Stinkerbell.

What's wet and brown and smells like peanuts?

Elephant puke.

A boy walks into a shop with a big pile of dog poo in his hand. He looks at the shopkeeper and says, "Phew. Look at that. To think I nearly stepped in it."

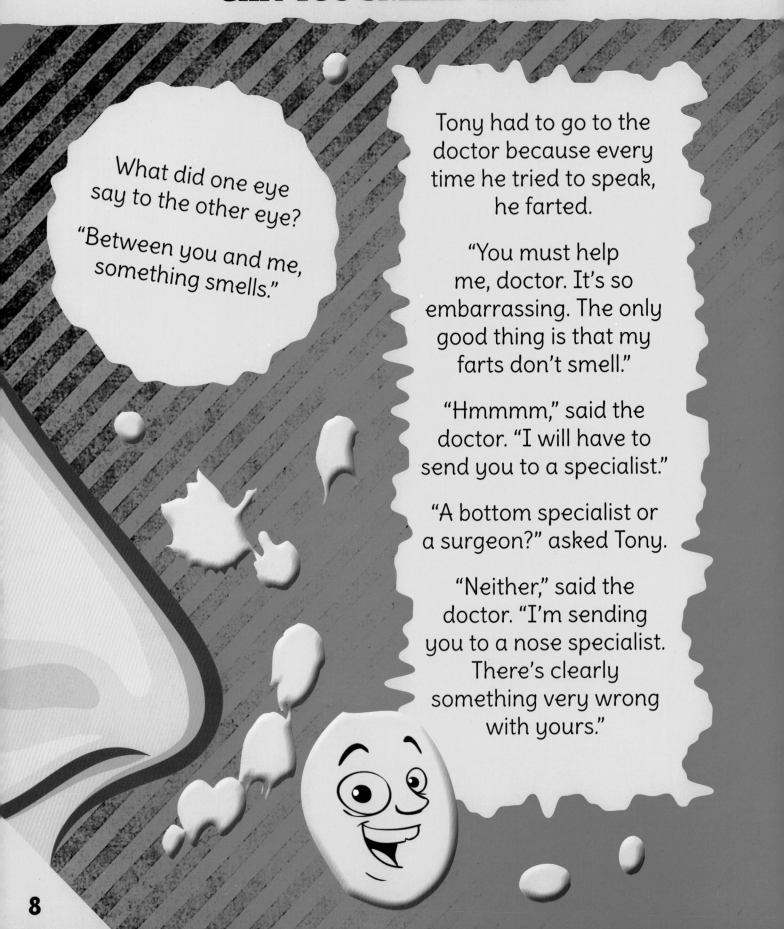

What did one eye say to the other eye?

"Between you and me, something smells."

Tony had to go to the doctor because every time he tried to speak, he farted.

"You must help me, doctor. It's so embarrassing. The only good thing is that my farts don't smell."

"Hmmmm," said the doctor. "I will have to send you to a specialist."

"A bottom specialist or a surgeon?" asked Tony.

"Neither," said the doctor. "I'm sending you to a nose specialist. There's clearly something very wrong with yours."

A belch is just one
gust of wind,
That comes straight
from the heart,
But should it take the
downward route,
It turns into a fart.

What did one plant say
to the other plant?

"You smell like you just
soiled yourself."

What's the smelliest
city in America?

Poo York.

How many rotten
eggs does it take to
make a stink bomb?

A phew.

What's the sharpest thing in the world?

A fart. It goes through your trousers and doesn't even leave a hole.

Doug: "My dog doesn't have a nose."

Matt: "Really? How does he smell?"

Doug: "Just awful."

Why do giraffes have such long necks?

Because they have smelly feet.

What do you call the smelliest queen in the world?

The Queen of Farts.

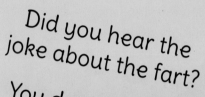

Did you hear the joke about the fart?

You don't want to. It stinks.

What did the skunk say when the wind changed direction?

"It's all coming back to me now."

What's huge, green and smelly?

The Incredible Hulk when he farts.

"Doctor, doctor, I'm going bald. Do you have anything to cure it?"

"Yes, put one pound of horse poo on your head every single morning."

"Will that make my hair grow back?"

"No, but no one will come close enough to see that you don't have any hair."

What's brown and smelly and sits on a piano stool?

Beethoven's last movement.

Did you hear about the slow student with terrible gas?

His parents hired a tooter.

Why did the beach smell like urine?

Because the sea weed.

What's the best way to keep flies out of your bathroom?

Poo in the hallway.

On what day of the week do most people get diarrhoea?

Splatter-day.

How do you stop a skunk from smelling?

Put a plug up its nose.

Where do burgers go to dance?

A meat ball.

If you are in assembly,
And your bottom
wants to shout,
Whatever you do,
Don't let it out.

What smells, runs around all day and lies around at night with its tongue hanging out?

A pair of old trainers.

What's green, sticky and smells gross?

An alien's nose.

What do you get if you cross a skunk with an owl?

Something that smells, but doesn't give a hoot.

SLIMY

Slime is funny. Don't ask why.
It just is. Slugs and slime go together
like poo and farts. Now that's gross.
Don't even get us started on snot.

What did the
slug say as he slid
down the wall?

"How slime flies."

Why was the
nose so tired?

Because it never
stopped running.

GROSS JOKES

What did the teacher say to the student whose homework was covered in slime?

"Your work is getting sloppy."

What did the spider say to the slug?

"It's about slime you showed up."

Anna thought the green flecks on the wall were paint.

Now we know it's snot.

How do you know your kitchen floor is dirty?

The slugs leave a trail on the floor that reads 'clean me'.

SLIMY

What do you
do when two snails
have a fight?

Leave them
to slug it out.

What is the
difference between
a prince and a bogey?

The prince is the
heir to the throne,
but the bogey is
thrown to the air.

How do snails get
their shells so shiny?

They use
snail varnish.

How do you
cure dandruff?

Cut off your head.

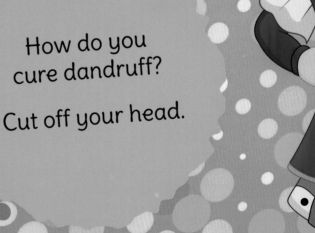

Don't kiss your honey,
When your nose
is runny.
You may think it's funny,
But it's snot.

What is the
definition of a slug?

A snail with a
housing problem.

What was the snail
doing on the road?

About one
mile a day.

What do blobs like
to drink the most?

Slime-ade.

What has 30,000 square miles, lies north of England and is green and slimy?

The country of Snotland.

What did the oyster call his oyster wife?

Shelley.

What do oysters say to their friends on the phone?

"Shello."

Who directed the film Snot Wars?

George Mucus.

Why did the bogey cross the road?

He was getting picked on.

What kind of bugs live in clocks?

Ticks.

What's another name for a snail?

A bogey wearing a crash helmet.

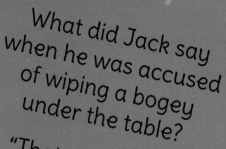

What did Jack say when he was accused of wiping a bogey under the table?

"That s'not mine."

What do you call snot that haunts you?

BOOgey.

Why was the glow-worm confused?

She didn't know if she was coming or glowing.

How do you make a tissue dance?

Put a little bogey into it.

What is gross, slimy and stuck between sharks' teeth?

Slow swimmers.

What's green and wobbly and hangs from trees?

Monkey snot.

Why do gorillas have big nostrils?

Because they have big fingers.

What is it called when someone gets hit in the face with slime?

Goo-lash.

Aaron: "Did you just pick your nose?"

Doug: "No, I was born with it."

Why are basketball players so messy?

Because they're always dribbling.

What is a cow's snot called?

Moo-cus.

Why do bees have sticky hair?

Because they use honey combs.

MONSTER JOKES

Monsters don't have to be scary.
Instead, they can be hilarious.
From Frankenstein's monster to
spooky ghosts, there are lots of jokes
about these terrifying creatures.

What's more gross than
three dead monsters
in a rubbish bin?

One dead monster
in three rubbish bins.

What do you call a
monster with no neck?

The Lost Neck Monster.

What happened
when the alien
ate uranium?

He got atomic ache.

GROSS JOKES

How did Frankenstein's monster sit in a chair?

Bolt upright.

Why did Frankenstein's monster get indigestion?

He bolted down his food.

Why is it foolish to upset a cannibal?

You will find yourself in hot water.

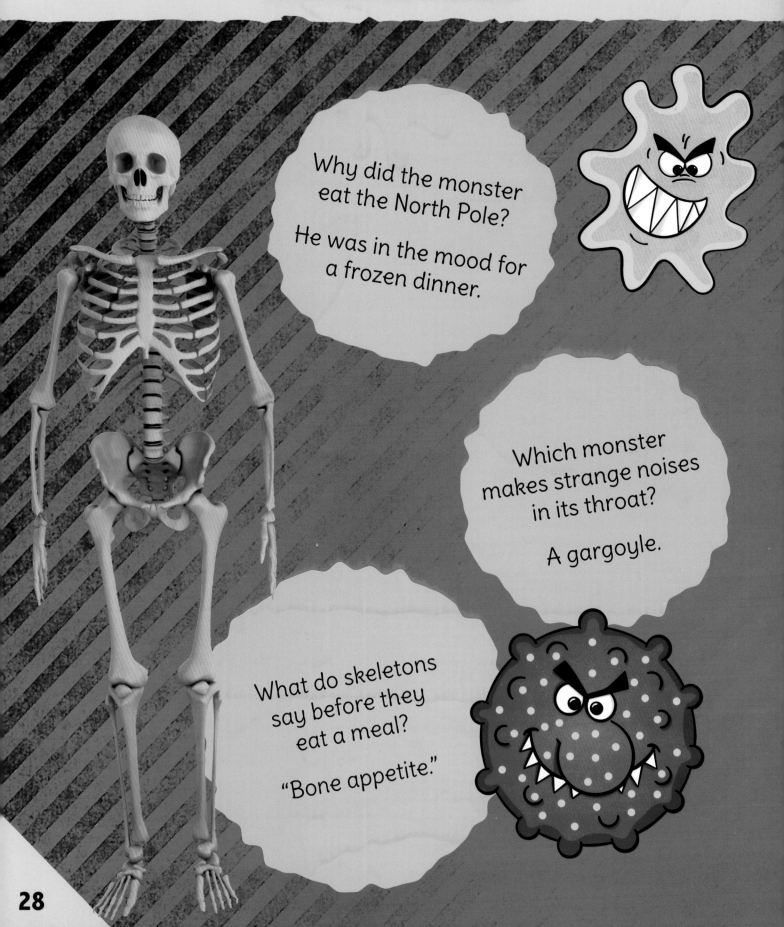

Why did the monster eat the North Pole?

He was in the mood for a frozen dinner.

Which monster makes strange noises in its throat?

A gargoyle.

What do skeletons say before they eat a meal?

"Bone appetite."

GROSS JOKES

What would you get if you crossed a practical joker with a mad scientist?

Dr Prankenstein.

What do you call a corpse who won't stop ringing your doorbell?

A dead ringer.

What did the cannibal say to her kids at the dinner table?

"Don't talk with people in your mouth."

What do cannibals do at a wedding?

Toast the bride and groom.

MONSTER JOKES

Why did the alien have a bath?

So he could make a clean getaway.

How can you help a starving cannibal?

Give him a hand.

Who created the fowlest monster in the world?

Ducktor Frankenstein.

What's green and fluffy and comes from Mars?

A martianmallow.

Why is Frankenstein's monster such a good gardener?

Because he has green fingers.

GROSS JOKES

Why are most mummies vain and conceited?

They're all wrapped up in themselves.

What do you do with a green monster?

Wait until it ripens.

What do you call a scary movie about a monster who takes money?

The Bribe of Frankenstein.

Monster: "Will this hurt?"

Dr Frankenstein: "Let's just say you're in for a big shock."

What did the cannibal say after he ate the circus clown?

"Boy, that sure tasted funny."

What type of music does a mummy like the most?

Wrap.

What did one casket say to the other?

"Is that you, coffin?"

Was Dracula ever married?

No, he was a bat-chelor.

What do you get when you cross a ghost with a firecracker?

Bam-boo.

Did you hear about the monster with five legs?

No, but I bet his trousers fit him like a glove.

Where do baby monsters go when their parents are at work?

Day scare.

What do big, scary monsters do to cars?

They make traffic jam.

What did the monster say about his eight arms?

"They come in handy."

What do ghosts like reading in newspapers?

Horror-scopes.

Where should a greedy, 500-pound monster go?

On a diet.

GRIMY AND SICK

Some subjects are gross and grimy. They can be sticky and icky or gross and dirty. Puke is all of those things at the same time. Eeewww!

Birdy, birdy in the sky, Dropped some white stuff in my eye. I'm a big boy, I won't cry. I'm just glad that cows don't fly.

A minister was asked to dinner by one of his parishioners, whom he knew was an unkempt housekeeper. When he sat down at the table, he noticed that the dishes were the dirtiest dishes he had ever seen.

"Were these dishes ever washed?" he asked his hostess, running his fingers over the grit and grime.

She replied, "They're as clean as soap and water could get them."

He felt quite apprehensive, but, not wanting to offend, he blessed the food anyway and started eating. It was really delicious and he said so, despite the dirty dishes.

When dinner was over, the hostess took the dishes to the dogs outside and yelled, "Here, Soap. Here, Water."

What's brown and sticky?

A stick.

What is red with green spots?

I don't know, but whatever it is, it just crawled behind your ear.

Why do maggots
eat vomit?

It's a dirty job, but
someone's got to do it.

What's yellow and
smells of dead people?

Cannibal puke.

What has four legs,
a tail and flies?

A dead horse.

Why do mother birds puke in their babies' mouths?

They want to send them out with a hot breakfast.

Mum: "Why did you put a frog in your sister's bed?"

John: "I couldn't find a snake."

What's brown and sounds like a bell?

Dung.

What's Mozart doing in his grave?

He's de-composing.

Why were the teacher's eyes crossed?

She couldn't control her pupils.

What did the man say when his vomit missed the bucket?

"Now that's beyond the pail."

Where do frogs get changed?

In a croakroom.

What kind of cake do you get at a bad cafe?

A stomach-cake.

What do you call a surgeon with eight arms?

A doctopus.

What shouldn't you drink when you have the flu?

Cough-ee.

What TV show did the puke like to watch?

Wallace and Vomit.

What do you call a crazy flea?

A loony-tic.

What illness do martial artists get?

Kung Flu.

What sound does a nut make when it sneezes?

"Cashew!"

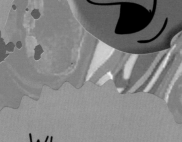

What did one escalator say to the other escalator?

"I think I'm coming down with something."

What time should you visit the dentist?

Tooth-hurty.

Dave: "Sir, my nose is running."

Teacher: "Well, chase after it."

Why did the bird go to the hospital?

To get tweeted.

What did the chicken say when it laid a square egg?

"Ouch."

How does a pig get to the hospital?

In a hambulance.

What do you call a dog with the runs?

A poodle.

Did you hear about the bird that acts crazy?

He's stork raving mad.

What did the dentist ask her husband when he baked a cake?

"Can I do the filling?"

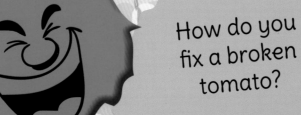

How do you fix a broken tomato?

With tomato paste.

What do you give a dog with a fever?

Mustard.
It's the best thing for a hot dog.

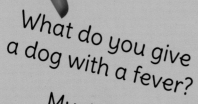

Why did the banana peel?

Because it didn't wear sunscreen.

Patient: "Doctor, doctor, I swallowed food dye."

Doctor: "You'll be okay."

Patient: "But I feel like I dyed a little inside."

What's in space, has feathers and farts a lot?

An Unidentified Farting Ostrich.

What did the astronaut call his poo in outer space?

A floater.

Why didn't the girl tell the doctor that she ate some glue?

Her lips were sealed.

GROSS TONGUE-TWISTERS

These tongue-twisters will have your tongue going in all directions. They are not jokes like in the rest of this book, but they will sound funny and silly and when you think about the words, you might get grossed out. You'll definitely have to reach into your mouth and untwist your tongue.

Six slippery snails slid slowly seaward.

I need not your needles, they're needless to me, For kneading of noodles was needless, you see.

Did my neat knickers need to be kneed? I then should have need of your needles indeed.

Freshly fried fat flying fish.

If a black bug bleeds black blood, what blood does a blue bug bleed?

A skunk sat on a stump and the stump thought the skunk stunk. The skunk thought the stump stunk. So, what stunk: the skunk or the stump?

GROSS TONGUE-TWISTERS

The ochre ogre ogled the poker.

How many seals did the seal slicer slice since the seal slicer shan't slice slippery seals?

Which rich wicked witch wished a wicked wish about another rich wicked witch?

I stepped on a stump and stomped on it, then I had a scratch that turned into a sore.

I feel a funny feel. A funny feel I feel. If you feel the feel I feel, then I feel the feel you feel.

A big, black bug bit a big, black bear and the big, black bear bled blood.

If Stu chews shoes, should Stu choose the shoes he chews?

Andrew and Arthur ate awful, acidic apples accidentally.

Francis fries foul fish fillets.

Brad's big, black bath brush broke.

Betty Botter had some butter. "This butter's bitter," she said. "If I bake this bitter butter, it would make my batter bitter, but a bit of better butter, that would make my batter better."

The rat-catchers can't catch caught rats.

If Freaky Fred found fifty feet of fruit and fed forty feet to his friend, Frank, how many feet of fruit did Freaky Fred find in the first place?

When a doctor pukes everywhere and another doctor doctors him, does the doctor doing the doctoring have to doctor the doctor the way the doctor being doctored wants to be doctored, or does the doctor doing the doctoring of the doctor doctor the doctor as he wants to do the doctoring?

There was an old lady from Ryde, Who drank apple cider and died. The apples fermented, Inside the lamented, And made cider inside her insides.

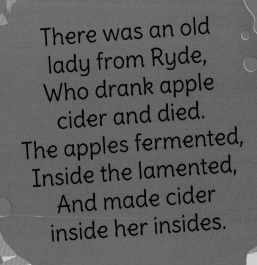

GROSS TONGUE-TWISTERS

The sloth loafs among the low slopes.

Three fiddling pigs sat in a pit and fiddled.

Fiddle, piggy, fiddle, piggy, fiddle, piggy.

The savour of the silly scent the sentry sent to Millicent.

How many slim, slimy snakes would slither silently to the sea if slim, slimy snakes could slither silently?

Amidst the mists and coldest frosts, With stoutest wrists and loudest boasts, He thrust his fists against the posts, And still insists he sees the ghosts.

Around the rugged rocks the ragged rascal ran.

Plague-bearing prairie dogs. Plague-bearing prairie dogs.

Crisp crusts crackle crunchily.

I cannot bear
to see a bear,
Bear down upon a hare.
When bare of hair, he
strips the hare,
Right there, I cry,
"Forbear!"

Flee from fog to fight flu fast.

Theo's throat throbs and thumps, thumps and throbs.

Many an anemone sees an enemy anemone.

Sixty-six sticky skeletons. Sixty-six sticky skeletons. Sixty-six sticky skeletons.

Horrible Heidi hears hairy Horace holler.

She stood on the balcony, inexplicably mimicking him hiccupping and amicably welcoming him home.

The epitome of femininity.

A selfish shellfish smelt a stale fish. If the stale fish was smelt, then the selfish shellfish smelt a smell.

Girl gargoyle, guy gargoyle.

FOOD GONE BAD

Fresh food is delicious, but even delicious food can be made totally, horribly gross. Animals can make a home in your food and mould can grow in it. Eeeuurrgh!

What vegetable might you find in your basement?

Cellar-y.

What's worse than finding a worm in your apple?

Finding half a worm.

Waiter: "What will you have to follow the roast pork, sir?"

Alex: "Indigestion, I expect."

Jake: "What's the difference between dog poo and chocolate?"

Mick: "I don't know."

Jake: "In that case, don't ever buy me chocolate."

Why did the orange stop in the middle of the road?

He ran out of juice.

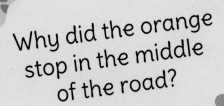

What do you call a cow on the floor of the barn?

Ground beef.

Brian: "Waiter, waiter, I simply can't eat this awful food. Get me the manager."

Waiter: "She won't eat it either."

A family of three tomatoes were walking down the street one day when the little baby tomato started lagging behind. The father tomato walked back to the baby tomato, stomped on her, squashing her into a red paste and said, "Ketch up."

What happened when the waiter tripped while carrying the intestines soup?

He spilled his guts.

What kind of peas are brown?

Poopeas.

What's the difference between a Brussels sprout and a bogey?

You can't get a kid to eat a Brussels sprout.

First egg: "I don't want to go in a pan of boiling water."

Second egg: "It gets worse. When they take you out, they bash your head in."

What's yellow and stupid?

Thick custard.

FOOD GONE BAD

Why did the banana go to the doctor?

Because it wasn't peeling well.

A guy walks into the doctor's office. He has a banana stuck in one of his ears, an asparagus stalk in the other ear and a carrot stuck in one nostril. The man says, "Doctor, this is terrible. What's wrong with me?"

The doctor says, "Well, first of all, you need to eat more sensibly."

First apple: "You look down in the dumps. What's eating you?"

Second apple: "Worms, I think."

Patrick: "Waiter, waiter, be careful. Your thumb is in my soup."

Waiter: "Not to worry. It isn't very hot."

Wife: "I thought you were trying to get in shape."

Husband: "I am. The shape I've chosen is a circle."

Tom: "Waiter, waiter, this egg is bad."

Waiter: "Don't blame me, I only laid the table."

What can a whole apple do that half an apple can't do?

Look round.

FOOD GONE BAD

A young man entered the ice-cream shop and asked, "What kind of ice cream do you have?"

"Vanilla, chocolate, strawberry," the girl wheezed. She patted her chest and seemed unable to continue.

"Do you have laryngitis?" the young man asked.

"Nope," she whispered. "Just vanilla, chocolate and strawberry."

Harry: "Waiter, waiter, there's a dead beetle in my drink."

Waiter: "Well, yes, the dead ones aren't very good swimmers."

What is the scariest fruit?

A boo-nana.

What did the chewing gum say to the shoe?

"I'm stuck on you."

GROSS JOKES

Why did the students eat their homework?

The teacher said it was a piece of cake.

What does a termite eat for breakfast?

Oak-meal.

What's green and white and jumps up and down?

A frog sandwich.

What fruit juice do ghosts like the most?

Lemon and slime.

What does an aardvark like on its pizza?

Ant-chovies.

FOOD GONE BAD

Jack: "Waiter, waiter, there's a cockroach in my salad."

Waiter: "Please don't shout or the other customers will ask for one, too."

Did you hear about the cannibal who was late for lunch?

He was given the cold shoulder.

What do zombies eat for breakfast?

Dreaded Wheat.

Want to hear a joke about pizza?

Never mind. It's too cheesy.

What did one maggot say to the other who was stuck in an apple?

"Try and worm your way out of that one."

Did you hear about the man who put his false teeth in backwards?

He ate himself.

Bob: "Waiter, waiter, why is your thumb on my steak?"

Waiter: "I don't want to drop it again."

What's the difference between roast chicken and pea soup?

You can roast chicken, but you can't pea soup.

Why do the French like to eat snails?

Because they don't like fast food.

ANIMAL GROSSNESS

Animals can be really gross and these jokes will have you and your friends in stitches. They're silly and full of creepy-crawlies and other slithery and smelly animals.

How can you tell when a gorilla's been in the fridge?

There are hairs in the butter.

What do you call a bear with its ear cut off?

'B'.

What do you get if you cross a fish with a pig?

Wet and dirty.

What's the difference between a maggot and a cockroach?

Cockroaches crunch more when you eat them.

Why was the stable boy so busy?

Because his work kept piling up.

What do you call a bag of rats?

A rat bag.

What do you get if you cross a dog with a lion?

A terrified postman.

What does a cat say when you accidentally step on its tail?

Me-OW!

ANIMAL GROSSNESS

What did the leech say when there was no more blood left in the dead rat?

"This really sucks."

What do you do if you find a python on the toilet?

Wait until he's finished.

What's black, white and green?

A zebra with a runny nose.

What do you call a tired bug?

A sleepy-crawly.

Do you know what they say about a bird in the hand?

It'll poo on your wrist.

What do you get
if you walk under
a cow?

A pat on the head.

What do you
call a sleeping bull?

A bull-dozer.

What do you
get when you cross
a rooster, a dog and
something gross?

Cock-a-poodle-eeew.

What do you call
a bug that has worked
its way to the top?

Head louse.

What do you get if you cross a centipede with a homing pigeon?

A creepy-crawly that just keeps coming back.

How do fleas get around?

By itchhiking.

What do you get when you run over a parakeet with a lawnmower?

Shredded tweet.

GROSS JOKES

Steph: "Our dog is really lazy."

Natalie: "Why do you say that?"

Steph: "I was watering the garden yesterday and he never lifted a leg to help."

Why do maggots like open wounds?

They don't have to fight over who gets the scab.

What did one fly ask the other?

"Is this stool taken?"

What do you get if you cross a scorpion with a rose?

I don't know, but don't try smelling it.

What do you do if an elephant eats a rotten egg?

Get out of the way.

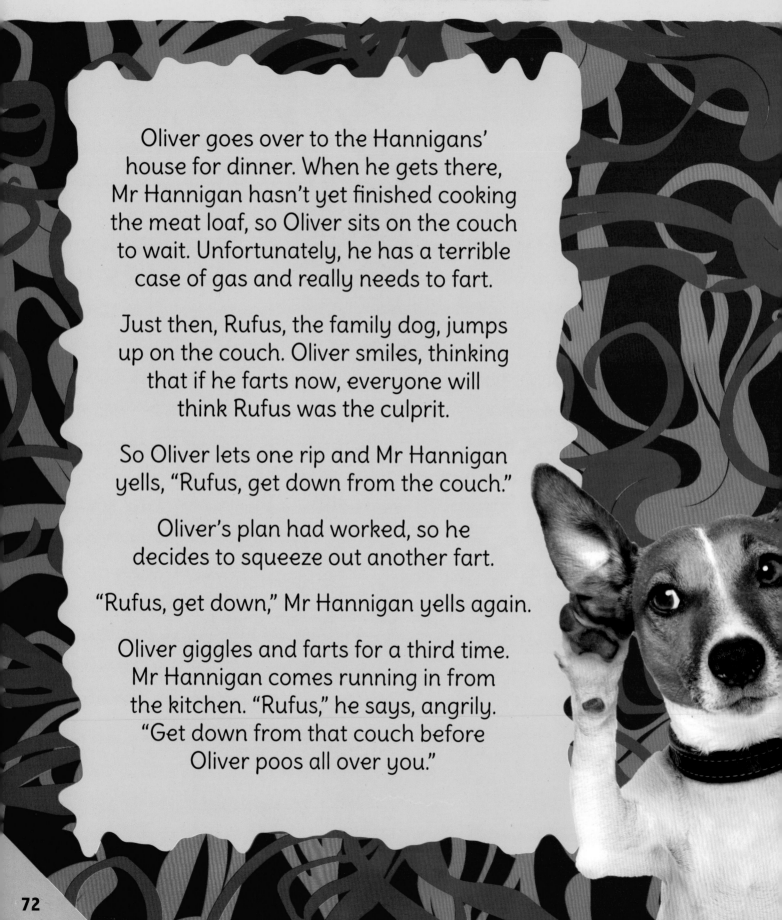

Oliver goes over to the Hannigans' house for dinner. When he gets there, Mr Hannigan hasn't yet finished cooking the meat loaf, so Oliver sits on the couch to wait. Unfortunately, he has a terrible case of gas and really needs to fart.

Just then, Rufus, the family dog, jumps up on the couch. Oliver smiles, thinking that if he farts now, everyone will think Rufus was the culprit.

So Oliver lets one rip and Mr Hannigan yells, "Rufus, get down from the couch."

Oliver's plan had worked, so he decides to squeeze out another fart.

"Rufus, get down," Mr Hannigan yells again.

Oliver giggles and farts for a third time. Mr Hannigan comes running in from the kitchen. "Rufus," he says, angrily. "Get down from that couch before Oliver poos all over you."

GROSS JOKES

How do you stop a cow from mooing loudly on Sunday morning?

Make beefburgers on Saturday night.

Why are frogs always so happy?

They eat whatever bugs them.

What do you get when you cross a chicken with a cement mixer?

A bricklayer.

Which day of the week do fish really hate?

Fry-day.

What did the grasshopper say when it hit the windscreen?

"I don't have the guts to do that again."

What do you get when you cross a cow with a camel?

Lumpy milkshakes.

Where do dogs go when they lose their tails?

To the re-tail shop.

How do you find where a flea has bitten you?

You start from scratch.

GROSS JOKES

What do you get when you cross a bug with a boot?

A squashed bug.

Which treat do cats like the most?

Chocolate mouse.

What did the dog say to the insect?

"Long time, no flea."

Why are elephants so wrinkly? Because they're too difficult to iron.

What do you get if you cross a worm and a young goat?

A dirty kid.

MWAH-HA-HA VILLAINS

We all love to hate a villain.
Their gross obsessions like sucking
blood and haunting buildings make
for funny jokes. Mwah-ha-ha!

What happened to Godzilla after he chewed through the streets of New York?

He came down with a sewer throat.

Which type of dog do ghosts like the most?

A ghoul-den retriever.

What has webbed feet and fangs?

Count Quackula.

What does a vampire order at the bar?

A Bloody Mary.

Why is Dracula's bank account always in the red?

Because it's a blood bank.

Who does Dracula always take to a party?

The girl necks door.

Why do vampires not have any friends?

Because they're a pain in the neck.

MWAH-HA-HA VILLAINS

What do you get when you cross a vampire with a snowman?

Frostbite.

What do ghosts like on their bagels?

Scream cheese.

What's green, crunchy and bites you on the neck?

A vampickle.

How do you know when a mummy has raided your fridge?

All the food is unwrapped.

How do vampires go sailing?

On blood vessels.

GROSS JOKES

What kind of streets do ghosts like to gather on?

Dead-end streets.

Who did Dracula invite to his wedding?

All his blood relatives.

Did you hear about the skeleton who went on a low-fat milk diet?

Now he's all skim and bones.

What do ghosts eat for dessert?

Ice scream.

How does Dracula like his food served?

In bite-sized pieces.

What does Dracula say before going out?

"I'm just popping out for a bite."

MWAH-HA-HA VILLAINS

What do vampires wear in autumn?

Their bat-to-school clothes.

What pets does Dracula own?

A bloodhound and a ghoulfish.

Why was the ghost so embarrassed?

He spook too soon.

What did the monster get when he won the race?

A ghoul medal.

Which flowers do ghouls like?

Morning gories.

What side of Godzilla should you stay away from?

The inside.

What kind of letters does Dracula get from admirers?

Fang mail.

What do you call a gremlin on crutches?

A hobblin' goblin.

Why are robots never afraid?

Because they have nerves of steel.

Why did the ghost cross the road?

To get to 'the other side.'

Do werewolves ever argue?

Whenever there's a full moon, they fight tooth and nail.

What did George say before his fight with a zombie?

"Do you want a piece of me?"

MWAH-HA-HA VILLAINS

Why did the zombie twins stay home from school?

They were feeling rotten.

How can you tell when a vampire has been in a bakery?

All the filling from the jam doughnuts is missing.

What's the most important day in Ancient Egypt?

Mummy's Day.

What do ghosts do on their days off?

Housecreeping.

Why did the art teacher praise Dracula?

Because he was good at drawing blood.

GROSS JOKES

What kind of sales attract zombies?

Graveyard sales.

Why did the vampire never gain weight?

He ate necks to nothing.

Why do ghosts make such poor football fans?

They spend all their time booing.

What kind of art are ghosts good at?

Ghoulages.

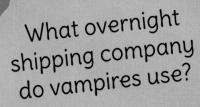

What happened when the vampires had a race?

They were neck and neck.

What overnight shipping company do vampires use?

Necks Day Delivery.

Who did the wizard marry?

His ghoulfriend.

What does Dracula do at the circus?

He goes straight for the juggler.

Why was the mummy so tense?

He was all wound up.

What do baby monsters eat?

Alpha-bat soup.

What can you find between Godzilla's toes?

Slow runners.

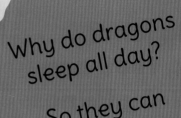

Why do dragons sleep all day?

So they can fight knights.

When do mummies eat breakfast?

When they catch you.

What happened when the wizard turned a boy into a hare?

He wouldn't stop rabbiting on about it.

Why did the skeleton play the piano?

Because he didn't have an organ.

BURPS AND FARTS

**Who doesn't love a smelly joke?
Burps, belches, poo, armpits, feet and
farts are just some of the stinky things
that gross us out and make us snigger.**

Pardon me for
being so rude,
It was not me,
it was my food.
It just popped up
to say hello.
Now it's gone back
down below.

I sat next
to a duchess at tea,
And it was just as
I feared it would be.
Her rumbling abdominal
was simply phenomenal
And everyone thought it
was me.

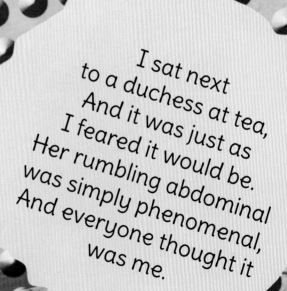

Brian: "I'm going to have to let one rip. Do you mind?"

Tom: "Not if you don't mind when I throw up."

How do you say "fart" in German?

Farfrompoopin.

How did the astronaut suffocate?

He farted in his spacesuit.

BURPS AND FARTS

What's the only kind of poo that doesn't smell terrible?

Shampoo.

Where is a fart on the spectrum?

Right after burple.

What is it called when a queen farts?

Noble gas.

How can you tell when your armpits are stinky?

Your teacher gives you an 'A' for not raising your hand in class.

What did one burp say to the other burp?

"Let's be stinkers and come out the other end."

How is a quiet fart like a ninja?

It's silent but deadly.

What did the queen bee do after she farted?

Issued a royal pardon.

How do you cope with a gas leak?

Leave the room and open all the windows.

Paul let out a huge, loud burp at a restaurant. A man at the next table said, "How dare you burp before my wife?" Paul replied, "I'm sorry. I didn't know she wanted to go first."

What's the easiest thing to break?

Wind.

GROSS JOKES

What do you call a knight who has just eaten baked beans?

Sir Farts-a-lot.

Did you hear about the man with explosive diarrhoea?

He had a fart attack.

What is invisible and smells like milk and biscuits?

Santa's burps.

Laugh and the whole world laughs with you. Fart and they'll stop laughing.

Rose: "Ewww, gross. Why did you just burp?"

Owen: "My fart got lonely."

What do you call a fart?

A turd honking for the right of way.

KNOCK-KNOCK.

Who's there?

Smell mop.

Smell mop who?

Ewww. What did you just say?

What did the judge say when the skunk walked in the courtroom?

"Odour in the court."

What do stinky toddlers learn at preschool?

Their one, poo, threes.

BURPS AND FARTS

What did the
stinky boy draw in his
Valentine's Day card?

Lovefarts.

What did the
bird say to its fart?

"You're the wind
beneath my wings."

Molly: "Mummy,
I hate my sister's guts."

Mum: "Well, stop eating
them, then."

What did the smelliest
married couple say in
their wedding vows?

"Till death do us fart."

GROSS JOKES

PIRATES AND WITCHES

There are some truly gross things about witches and pirates. Peg legs, warts, eyepatches, pointy nails and hook hands just for a start.

What is a male witch detective called?

Warlock Holmes.

GROSS JOKES

Where do pirates put their stuff at the gym?

In Davey Jones' locker.

What happened to the witch with an upside-down nose?

Every time she sneezed, her hat blew off.

What do you get if you cross a witch with an iceberg?

A cold spell.

Which weapons do pirates like the most?

Dagaaaaaarrrrrrs.

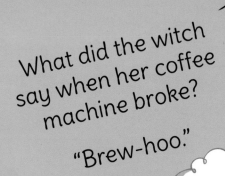

What did the witch say when her coffee machine broke?

"Brew-hoo."

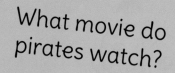

What movie do pirates watch?

Booty and the Beast.

What internet sensation is popular with pirates?

Planking.

What do witches excel at in school?

Spelling.

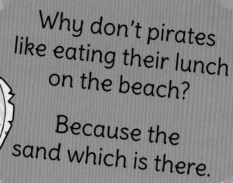

Why don't pirates like eating their lunch on the beach?

Because the sand which is there.

How does a pirate propose to his girlfriend?

"Yo, ho. Yo, ho. A pirate's wife for me?"

Why can't pirates learn the alphabet?

Because they insist there are 7 'Cs'.

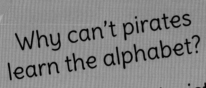

PIRATES AND WITCHES

A pirate was being interviewed about his life at sea. The interviewer began speaking. "So, Captain, how did you get your peg leg?"

"I fell one night and broke me ankle. The ship doesn't have a doctor, so we cut it off and put the leg on thar."

The reporter was disappointed, as she had expected a more exciting story. Her next question was about why he had a hook for a hand. He responded, "T'was me night to do the cookin' and I wasn't paying attention when cuttin' the food. As we didn't have no doctor to fix me up, we put the hook on thar instead."

Once again, the story had been less exciting than expected. The final question was about the patch on his eye, to which he explained, "I was out on the deck lookin' at the sea, when a seagull flew overhead. Its droppings fell clear into me eye."

The reporter was confused. "So that's why you wear a patch over your eye?"

The captain responded, "No, I tried to wipe off the poo with me hook."

What has four hands and four legs?

Eight pirates.

How much did the pirate pay for his peg leg and hook?

An arm and a leg.

Why did the angry witch land with a bump?

Because she lost her temper and flew off the handle.

PIRATES AND WITCHES

What do you get when you cross a sorceress with a billionaire?

A very witch person.

Why wouldn't the pirate's phone work?

He left it off the hook.

Why did the witch give up fortune telling?

She saw no future in it.

What do witches wear to bed?

Fright-gowns.

Why couldn't the witch sing Christmas carols?

Because of the frog in her throat.

How do witches tell the time?

With a witch watch.

Which side of a parrot has the prettiest feathers?

The outside.

Why are pirate flags always in a bad mood?

Because they have cross bones.

Why did the witch itch?

Someone took away the 'W'.

What did the pirate name his daughter?

Peggy.

What happened to the witch when she went to another country?

She got broom-sick.

Why couldn't the pirate play cards?

He was standing on the deck.

What happened to the naughty, little witch at school?

She got ex-spelled.

TOILET JOKES

The toilet is a ripe area for jokes. Just think of all the horrible, loud and smelly things that happen in the toilet. Get ready to laugh at the grossness of those stinky bathroom bowls.

Why did Tigger look in the toilet?

He was looking for Pooh.

Mel: "Do you know anyone who has been on the TV?"

Andrew: "My brother did once, but he uses the toilet now."

Why do idiots whistle when they go for a poo?

So they can remember which end to wipe.

Why did the boy take toilet paper to the birthday party?

Because he was a party pooper.

A boy with a bladder problem asked his teacher if he could go to the bathroom.

"Only if you recite the alphabet," answered the teacher.

"Okay," said the boy. "ABCDEFGHIJK LMNO - QRSTUV WXYZ."

"Where's the 'P'?" asked the teacher.

"Running down my leg," said the boy.

What did the first mate see in the spaceship's toilet?

The captain's log.

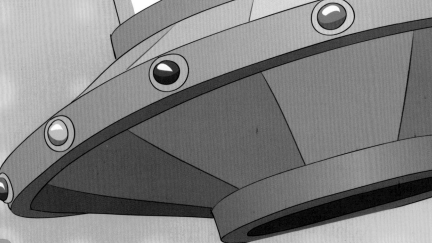

Why did the toilet paper roll down the hill?

Because it wanted to get to the bottom.

What did one piece of toilet paper say to the other piece?

"I can't tear myself away from you."

What did Shakespeare say when he was potty training?

"To pee or not to pee. That is the question."

Did you hear about the new head teacher who's been keeping the boys on their toes?

He raised all the urinals six inches.

What did the bath say when he thought the toilet was ill?

"You look flushed."

Turd 1: "I just got dumped."

Turd 2: "How are you feeling?"

Turd 1: "Like poo."

Why was the toilet paper unimpressed with the price?

It felt it was ripped off.

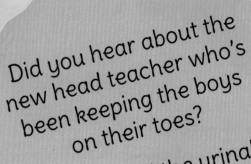

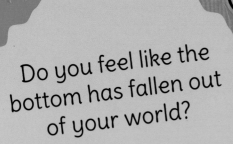

Do you feel like the bottom has fallen out of your world?

Eat prunes and then the world will fall out of your bottom.

What is a woman with two toilets on her head called?

Lulu.

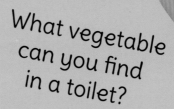

What vegetable can you find in a toilet?

A leek.

What happened when the girl ate too many Mexican jumping beans?

Her poo hopped right out of the toilet.

Carl: "Teacher, do farts have lumps in them?"

Teacher: "Um, no."

Carl: "Then I definitely just pooed my pants."

Jen entered a competition where the first prize was a toilet and the last prize was a toilet.

It was a win-loos situation.

Why did the man bring the bowling ball into the bathroom?

So he could watch his toilet bowl.

What's green and lives at the bottom of the toilet?

Kermit the bog.

Why did the mummy go to the toilet?

To wrap itself in toilet paper, of course.

Three boys were at the top of a slide when a genie appeared, saying it would grant each of them one wish, which would come true at the bottom of the slide. They just had to call out their wish as they went down the slide.

The first boy shouted, "Money!" as he went down the slide and he landed in a huge pile of money.

The second boy shouted, "Chocolate!" as he went down the slide and was surrounded by chocolate at the bottom.

The third boy forgot what the genie had said and exclaimed, "Weeeeee!" as he went down the slide... and he landed in a puddle of stinky, yellow wee.

SILLY JOKES

SILLY ANIMALS

Animals are truly funny creatures. These jokes will have your sides splitting and your ribs tickling.

Why did the fox cross the road?

To look for the chicken.

What food do hedgehogs like most?

Prickled onions.

What do you call
a bird in winter?

A brrrd.

Why did the goose
cross the road?

To have a gander
on the other side.

Haaaa!

Why couldn't
Bob ride a bike?

Because Bob's
a fish.

What do you
call a donkey with
only three legs?

A wonkey.

Ha!

How do you catch a squirrel?

Climb a tree and act like a nut.

Where do sheep get their hair cut?

At the baa-baas, of course.

Haaaa!

What kind of fish goes well with ice cream?

Jellyfish.

Which dance will a chicken not do?

The foxtrot.

What did the horse say when it fell?

"I've fallen and I can't giddy-up."

Ha!

SILLY JOKES

What do you call a bird that's out of breath?

A puffin.

Why are fish easy to weigh?

They have their own scales.

LOL!

What kind of animal goes, "Oom"?

A cow walking backwards.

How do you save a drowning mouse?

Give it mouse-to-mouse resuscitation.

HAaaa!

What did the parakeet say when he finished shopping?

"Just put it on my bill."

What does a farmer talk about when milking cows?

Udder nonsense.

LOL!

Ha! Hee Heeee!

What do you call a rooster who wakes up at the same time every morning?

An alarm cluck.

Why do seagulls fly over the sea?

If they flew over a bay, they'd be called bagels.

Why did the chicken join the band?

Because he had the drumsticks.

Ha!

What do you get if you pour boiling water down a rabbit hole?

A hot cross bunny.

How does a chicken tell the time?

One o'cluck, two o'cluck, three o'cluck.

Haaaa!

What do you get when a chicken lays an egg on top of a barn?

An egg roll.

What do you call a cow that eats your grass?

A lawn-mooer.

SILLY ANIMALS

Patient: "Doctor, doctor, I keep thinking I'm a sheep."

Doctor: "Really? How do you feel about that?"

Patient: "Really baaaaaaaaaadd."

What's the best way to brush your hair?

Hold him firmly by his long ears and brush gently.

Ha! Hee Heeee!

What do you get if you cross a hen with a dog?

Pooched eggs.

Ha!

Which animal keeps the best time?

A watchdog.

Why are elephants inappropriate when they go swimming?

They can't keep their trunks up.

LOL!

How do mice celebrate when they move into a new hole?

They have a mouse-warming party.

What did the farmer call his two rows of cabbages?

A dual cabbage way.

Haaaa!

What do you call a pony with a cough?

A little hoarse.

How does a dog stop a DVD?

He presses the paws button.

What is black and white and lives in Hawaii?

A lost penguin.

What would happen if pigs could fly?

The price of bacon would go up.

Did you hear about the pig with a rash?

He needed a little oinkment.

Why did the worm sleep in?

Because it didn't want to get caught by the early bird.

Who stole the soap?

The robber ducky.

What's black, white and green?

A seasick zebra.

Ha!

Ha! Hee Heeee!

Why don't centipedes play football?

By the time they put their shoes on, the game would be over.

SCARY AND SILLY

Get ready for some freaky frights with these silly, scary jokes. You will love making your friends cackle with these perfectly putrid puns.

LOL!

What do you call two witches who live together?

Broom-mates.

Ha! Hee Heeee!

What happened when the wizard met the witch?

It was love at first fright.

What kind of mistakes do ghosts make?

Boo-boos.

Why did Dracula take up acting?

It was in his blood.

Ha!

What kind of horses do ghosts ride in the dark?

Night mares.

What dessert do ghosts like the most?

Boo-berry pie.

Haaaa!

Why are skeletons always so calm?

Because nothing gets under their skin.

What should you say when meeting a ghost?

"How do you boo?"

Ha! Hee Heeee!

Why didn't Jason believe the ghost's lie?

Because he could see right through him.

SILLY JOKES

What did the ghost say to his girlfriend?

"You're boo-tiful."

What do you get when a vampire bites a plumber?

A bloodbath.

What did the alien say to the book?

"Take me to your reader."

Why should men be afraid of witches?

They'll be swept off their feet.

What sound does a witch's breakfast make?

Snap, cackle and pop.

Ha! Hee Heeee!

What scary creature writes invisible books?

A ghost writer.

Haaaa!

What do monsters eat for breakfast?

Devilled eggs.

What happened to Ray when he was eaten by a monster?

He became an ex-Ray.

Where do ghosts buy their food?

At the ghost-ery shop.

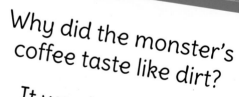

Why did the monster's coffee taste like dirt?

It was just ground this morning.

LOL!

Haaaa!

Which fruit do vampires like the most?

Neck-tarines.

Who gave the lecture at the ghost convention?

The spooksperson.

Ha!

Where is the best place to speak to a monster?

From a long way off.

What do you call a warlock who tries to stop fights?

A peacelock.

Why is the letter 'V' like a monster?

It comes after 'U'.

Where do ghosts and skeletons like to swim?

In the Dead Sea.

Haaaa!

Why did the witch put her broom in the washing machine?

Because she wanted a clean sweep.

When is it bad luck to see a black cat?

When you're a mouse.

LOL!

What party game do ghosts like to play?

Hide-and-shriek.

LOL!

Why do vampires need mouthwash?

Because they have bat breath.

Ha!

Which Spanish dance do vampires like?

The fangdango.

What did the skeleton order at the restaurant?

Spare ribs.

Haaaa!

Why are monsters so forgetful?

Because everything goes in one ear and out three others.

SPORTY SILLINESS

The sporting arena might not seem a likely place to set silly jokes, but just you wait. This chapter is full of silly, sporty fun.

Ha!

What sport do mosquitoes play?

Skin diving.

LOL!

Why did the team of artists never win a hockey match?

Because they kept drawing.

What has 22 feet and two wings, but can't fly?

A football team.

Why did the golfer pack an extra pair of trousers?

In case he got a hole in one.

Ha!

How do you start a flea race?

Say, "One, two, flea, go!"

Haaaa!

What sport do bees like to play?

Rug-bee.

How did the football pitch turn into a traingle?

Somebody took a corner

What sport do vampires play together?

Bat-minton.

Ha!

What do cricketers and magicians have in common?

They both do hat tricks.

Haaaa!

How do you make a cream puff?

Chase it around the garden.

SILLY JOKES

Why can't you play sports in the jungle?

Because there are too many cheetahs.

Ha!

What lights up a football stadium?

A football match.

Haaaa!

Why did the baseball coach spill the lemonade?

There was something wrong with the pitcher.

Which dessert does gymnastics?

The banana split.

How do hens encourage their football team?

They egg them on.

Haaaa!

Why are spiders such good swimmers?

Because they have webbed feet.

Why did the tightrope walker visit the bank?

To check his balance.

LOL!

Why didn't the dog want to play tennis?

Because he was a boxer.

What's the hardest part of skydiving?

The ground.

Haaaa!

Why shouldn't you tell jokes while ice skating?

Because the ice might crack up.

Why was Cinderella bad at basketball?

She ran away from the ball.

Ha!

Which insect makes a terrible goalkeeper?

The fumble bee.

Haaaa!

Would you ever go rock climbing?

I would if I was boulder.

What do you call a frozen bike?

B-b-b-bicycle.

Ha! Hee Heeee!

LOL!

Why couldn't Robin play cricket?

Because he lost his bat, man.

Why did the cricket team hire a cook?

They needed a good batter.

How can you stop squirrels from playing cricket in the garden?

Hide the ball. It drives them nuts.

LOL!

Why couldn't the bicycles stand up?

Because they were two tyred.

What did the baseball glove say to the baseball?

"Catch you later."

Why did all the bowling pins sit down?

Because they were on strike.

Ha!

Why did the football quit the team?

It was tired of being kicked around.

Why are fish bad at tennis?

Because they don't like getting close to the net.

Ha!

Why couldn't the tennis player light a fire?

Because he had lost all of his matches.

Why did the chicken get a red card?

Because of her fowl play.

LOL!

What kind of stories are told by basketball players?

Tall stories.

What tea do football players drink?

Penal-tea.

When is cricket a crime?

When there's a hit and run.

Ha! Hee Heeee!

Haaaa!

Which athlete stays the warmest?

The long jumper.

What happened to the man with a fear of hurdles?

He got over it.

SILLY BIRTHDAYS

Birthday parties are the perfect time to make your friends roll around with laughter. What's more fitting than telling them silly jokes about birthdays?

Ha! Hee Heeee!

LOL!

Johnny: "I get heartburn every time I eat birthday cake."

Mike: "Well, take the candles off next time."

Was anybody famous born on your birthday?

No, only babies were born on my birthday.

Ha!

Matt: "When's your birthday?"

Will: "22nd of March."

Matt: "What year?"

Will: "Every year."

What do you call an adult balloon?

A blown-up.

LOL!

What's the best kind of birthday present?

Another one.

Dylan: "Did you go to Megan's birthday?"

Sally: "No, the invite said '4 to 8' and I'm 9."

KNOCK-KNOCK.

Who's there?

Wanda.

Wanda who?

Wanda wish you a happy birthday.

Ha!

What did the big candle say to the little candle?

"You're too young to go out."

Sam: "Well, I guess my birthday wish didn't come true."

Amanda: "How do you know?"

Sam: "You're still here."

LOL!

How can you tell that birthdays are good for you?

Statistics show that people with the most birthdays live the longest.

Haaaa!

Ha! Hee Heeee!

KNOCK-KNOCK.

Who's there?

Abby.

Abby who?

Abby Birthday to you.

What do you get every birthday?

A year older.

Why do we put candles on the top of birthday cakes?

Because it would be too hard to put them on the bottom.

Ha!

HAaaa!

What does every happy birthday end with?

The letter 'Y'.

What is the left side of a birthday cake?

The side that's not eaten.

LOL!

Why did Emma stand on her head at the birthday party?

They were having upside-down cake.

Did you hear about the tree's birthday?

It was a sappy one.

Ha! Hee Heeee!

What do you say to a cow on her birthday?

"Happy birthday to moo."

Ha!

Haaaa!

Why did Tommy hit his birthday cake with a hammer?

It was a pound cake.

What did the birthday cake say to the ice cream?

"You're cool!"

LOL!

LOL!

What did the elephant wish for on his birthday?

A trunkful of presents.

What did the ice cream say to the unhappy cake?

"Hey, what's eating you?"

Ha! Hee Heeee!

Ha!

What did one candle say to another candle?

"Don't birthdays burn you up?"

What did the birthday balloon say to the pin?

"Hi, Buster."

LOL!

What does a clam do on his birthday?

He shellabrates.

LOL!

Haaaa!

What type of birthday cake did the elf eat?

Shortcake.

What was the average age of a caveman?

Stone Age.

SILLY BIRTHDAYS

What has wings, a long tail and wears a bow?

A birthday pheasant.

Ha!

Ha! Hee Heeee!

Where do you find a birthday present for a cat?

In a cat-alogue.

Haaaa!

What party game do rabbits like to play?

Musical hares.

Why was the birthday cake as hard as a rock?

It was marble cake.

154

What kind of music do balloons hate?

Pop music.

Does a pink candle burn longer than a blue one?

No, they both burn shorter.

LOL!

LOL!

Joel: "Why didn't you get me anything for my birthday?"

Zach: "You told me to surprise you."

SILLY OUTER SPACE

These silly jokes about outer space are truly out of this world. Get ready to blast off into a galaxy of the silliest jokes you could possibly imagine.

LOL!

Why do aliens not celebrate Christmas?

They don't like to share their presence.

HAaaa!

What holds the moon up in the sky?

Moonbeams.

Why did the scientist disconnect his doorbell?

He wanted to win the No-bell Prize.

How do you get a baby astronaut to sleep?

Rock-et.

Ha!

LOL!

Where do Martians go for a drink?

Mars bars.

What did E.T's parents say to him when he got home?

"Where on Earth have you been?"

Haaaa!

What did Mars say to Saturn?

"Give me a ring some time."

What did the astronaut see in the frying pan?

An unidentified frying object.

Ha! Hee Heeee!

How does a Martian know he's attractive?

When bits of metal stick to him.

Why don't astronauts get hungry after being blasted into space?

Because they just had a big launch.

Haaaa!

What game do spacemen play?

Astronauts and crosses.

Ha!

Where do aliens leave their flying saucers?

At parking meteors.

Haaaa!

Ha!

How did the solar system keep its trousers up?

With an asteroid belt.

Why did the spaceship land outside the bedroom?

Someone had left the landing light on.

LOL!

Why did the Martian go to the optician?

He had stars in his eyes.

HAaaa!

Why did the alien wear a bulletproof vest?

Because of all the shooting stars.

What do you call a wizard from outer space?

A flying sorcerer.

Ha!

What did the alien say to the gardener?

"Take me to your weeder."

LOL!

What did one shooting star say to the other?

"Pleased to meteor."

Where do aliens keep their sandwiches?

In a launch box.

LOL!

How does the moon cut his hair?

Eclipse it.

Ha!

What happened when Sam met an alien cat?

He had a close encounter with the furred kind.

How do you know
when the moon has
had enough to eat?

When it's full.

Why did the sun
go to school?

To get brighter.

What do planets
like to read?

Comet books.

What do you call
a tick on the moon?

A luna-tick.

What key do astronauts like to press on their computer keyboards?

The space bar.

Why did the cow go to outer space?

To visit the Milky Way.

Ha!

What was the first animal in space?

The cow that jumped over the moon.

What do you call an overweight alien?

An extra-cholesterol.

Why didn't people like the restaurant on the moon?

Because it had no atmosphere.

Haaaa!

What do aliens wear to weddings?

Their space-suits.

How many astronomers does it take to change a light bulb?

None. Astronomers aren't scared of the dark.

How do astronauts serve dinner?

On flying saucers.

Ha!

Why didn't the sun go to university?

Because it already had a million degrees.

Ha! Hee Heeee!

What do you get if you cross Santa with a spaceship?

U-F-ho-ho-ho.

How do you get ready for a space party?

You planet.

LOL!

THE SILLY HUMAN BODY

The human body can do truly amazing things, but it can also do truly hilarious things, too. There's a reason we all have a funny bone!

What has a bottom at its top?

A leg.

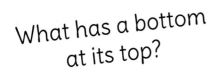

Haaaa!

Ha!

What happened when the two red blood cells fell in love?

They loved in vein.

What should you do if you split your sides laughing?

Run until you get a stitch.

Ha!

LOL!

Tom: "I just swallowed a bone."

Ian: "Are you choking?"

Tom: "No, I'm serious."

Where did the Egyptian mummy go to get her back fixed?

The Cairo-practor.

Ha! Hee Heeee!

LOL!

What did one ear say to the other?

"Between us, we have brains."

How long can you live without a brain?

Well, how old are you?

LOL!

Patient: "Doctor, doctor, I think I'm a battery."

Doctor: "How do you feel about it?"

Patient: "Well, it has its pluses and minuses."

What makes music on your hair?

A headband.

What's the most musical bone?

The trom-bone.

Ha!

Patient: "Doctor, doctor, I've lost my memory."

Doctor: "When did this happen?"

Patient: "When did what happen?"

Haaaa!

What's the best thing to put in a pie?

Your teeth.

What do you call a woman with one leg longer than the other?

I-lean.

Haaaa!

Why aren't snakes easy to fool?
You can't pull their leg.

LOL!

What do you call a man with no arms and no legs, as he floats down a river?

Bob.

Billy: "I don't think I need a spine."

Lucy: "Why is that?"

Billy: "It's holding me back."

LOL!

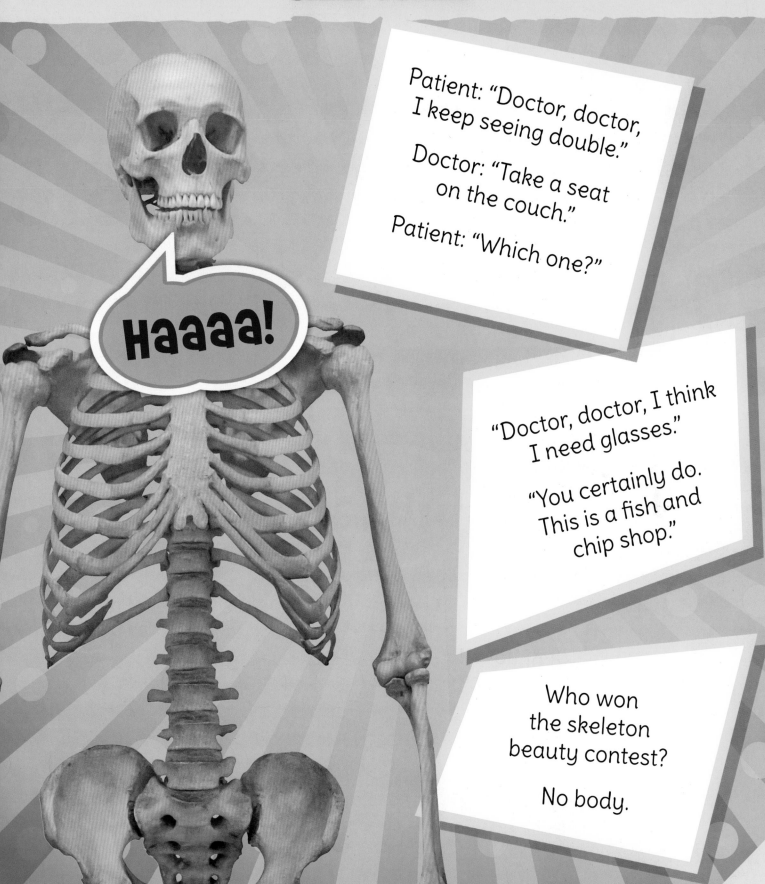

Patient: "Doctor, doctor, I keep seeing double."

Doctor: "Take a seat on the couch."

Patient: "Which one?"

"Doctor, doctor, I think I need glasses."

"You certainly do. This is a fish and chip shop."

Who won the skeleton beauty contest?

No body.

Pete: "Doctor, doctor, I got a strawberry stuck up my bum."

Doctor: "You're in luck. I have some cream for that."

What kind of flower grows on your face?

Two lips.

Why do skeletons hate winter?

Because the cold goes right through them.

What do you call a skeleton who won't get up in the mornings?

Lazy bones.

How did the skeleton know it was going to rain?

She could feel it in her bones.

Why do skeletons like to drink milk?

Because milk is so good for the bones.

Ha! Hee Heeee!

LOL!

What should you do if your nose goes on strike?

Picket.

Hannah: "Do you ever file your nails?"

Beth: "No, I throw them away immediately."

Why can't a nose be 12 inches long?

Because then it'd be a foot.

LOL!

LOL!

Haaaa!

What do you call a judge with no thumbs?

Justice Fingers.

Why did the one-handed man cross the road?

To get to the second-hand shop.

LOL!

What did the boy with bad teeth do when he went on a rollercoaster?

He braced himself.

Ha!

DINOSAUR SILLINESS

It has been a long time since dinosaurs ruled the Earth and we don't know if they liked silly jokes or not. Given how cool they looked, we think they must have.

Haaaa!

What has a spiky tail and sixteen wheels?

A stegosaurus on roller skates.

Ha!

Why did the dinosaur bathe?

To get ex-stinked.

What do you get when a dinosaur sneezes?

Out of the way.

Ha!

What followed the dinosaurs?

Their tails.

LOL!

What mark did the dinosaur get in his exam?

Extinction.

What do you call a blind dinosaur?

Do-you-think-he-saurus.

Haaaa!

DINOSAUR SILLINESS

What do you call a dinosaur wearing tight shoes?

My-foot-is-saurus.

Why did the dinosaur cross the road?

Because the chicken didn't exist yet.

Ha!

What does a T-rex eat?

Anything he wants.

What does a dinosaur get from scrubbing floors?

Dino-sores.

LOL!

Why are there old dinosaur bones in the museum?

Because they can't afford to buy new ones.

Which is the scariest dinosaur?

The terror-dactyl.

What do you call a dinosaur that won't stop talking?

A dino-bore.

Ha!

LOL!

What should you never ask a T-rex to do?

Clap.

SILLY JOKES

How did the dinosaur feel after eating a pillow?

A little bit down in the mouth.

Ha!

What did the triceratops sit on?

His tricera-bottom.

LOL!

What should you do if you see a blue dinosaur?

Try to cheer him up.

What do you get when dinosaurs crash their cars?

Tyrannosaurus wrecks.

DINOSAUR SILLINESS

What do you call a dinosaur that likes playing with blocks?

Stack-o-saurus.

What was the dinosaurs' lucky number?

Ate.

LOL!

HAaaa!

What did the caveman say when he slid down the dinosaur's neck?

"So long."

How do you invite a dinosaur to dinner?

"Tea, Rex?"

What makes more noise than a dinosaur?

Two dinosaurs.

How did the dinosaur blow up her garage?

With dino-mite.

Ha!

What do you call a dinosaur that never gives up?

Try-hard-ceratops.

Why did the T-rex like to eat snowmen?

Because they melted in his mouth.

What happened when the diplodocus took the train home?

He had to bring it back.

What's smarter than a talking dinosaur?

A spelling bee.

What did the brontosaurus say to the pterodactyl?

"Why the long face?"

What brand of T-shirts do dinosaurs wear?

Tricera-tops.

Ha!

LOL!

What did the doctor say to the invisible dinosaur?

"Sorry, I can't see you right now."

How can you tell there's a stegosaurus in your fridge?

The door won't close.

Haaaa!

FOOD IS SILLY

Food, glorious food. It's delicious and hilarious and very silly. Take a bite out of this special brand of silliness.

How do you know that carrots are good for your eyes?

Because you never see rabbits wearing glasses.

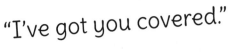
LOL!

LOL!

What did the apple skin say to the apple?

"I've got you covered."

Why did the man get fired from the banana factory?

Because he threw out all the bent ones.

Ha!

What type of nut is made from bread?

A doughnut.

LOL!

Why was the man swimming in a bowl of muesli?

A strong currant had pulled him in.

Why did the jelly wobble?

Because it saw the milk shake.

Why did the bacon laugh?

Because the egg cracked a yolk.

Why did the idiot eat biscuits?

He was crackers.

What do sea monsters eat?

Fish and ships.

Ha! Hee Heeee!

LOL!

What do you call shoes made from banana peels?

Slippers.

What do you call cheese that isn't yours?

Nacho cheese.

What do drummers have for dinner?

Chicken drumsticks.

What did the green grape say to the purple grape?

"Breathe! Breathe!"

Haaaa!

Why did the cucumber need a lawyer?

Because she was in a pickle.

What did baked beans do to Doug's intestines?

They rectum.

Where do baby apes sleep?

In apricots.

Haaaa!

What did one plate say to the other plate?

"Lunch is on me."

Did you hear the joke about the butter?

I won't tell you because it might spread.

LOL!

How do you make a mouse smile?

Say, "Cheese!"

SILLY JOKES

What kind of keys do kids like to carry?

Cookies.

What do you call an angry pea?

Grump-pea.

LOL!

What do sheep have for Christmas lunch?

Baa-becue food.

What's red, squishy and goes round and round?

A tomato stuck in a revolving door.

Why did the boy throw butter into the sky?

He wanted to see a butterfly.

Why couldn't the burger stop making jokes?

It was on a roll.

What kind of bear has a sweet tooth?

A gummy bear.

What is square and green?

A lemon in disguise.

Why aren't bananas ever lonely?

Because they come in bunches.

What do you call a retired vegetable?

A has-bean.

LOL!

Which vegetable goes best with jacket potatoes?

Button mushrooms.

Why did the tomato go out with the prune?

Because he couldn't find a date.

Ha!

How can you make a chicken stew?

Keep it waiting for hours.

What did the tin say to the tin opener?

"You make me flip my lid."

Why did the apple cry?

Its peelings were hurt.

LOL!

How do you make a banana split?

Cut it in half.

Why did the cookie go to the hospital?

He felt crumby.

What did the toaster say to the loaf?

"Pop up and see me sometime."

What did the mayonnaise say to the fridge?

"Go away. I'm dressing."

Why do basketball players like bisuits?

Because you can dunk them.

Ha!

What cheese is made backwards?

Edam.

Why are cows so poor?

Because farmers milk them dry.

Haaaa!

HOW SILLY IS HISTORY?

History may have happened a long time ago, but that doesn't make it any less hysterical.

Ha! Hee Heeee!

How do you use an Ancient Egyptian doorbell?

Toot and come in.

LOL!

Why did Robin Hood only rob the rich?

Because the poor didn't have anything worth stealing.

Which civilisation invented the fountain pen?

The Inkas.

Who was the fastest runner in history?

Adam. He was first in the human race.

Where did the pilgrims land when they came to America?

On their feet.

LOL!

What was the speed limit in Ancient Egypt?

Forty Niles an hour.

What do you get if you cross the Atlantic with the Titanic?

Halfway.

Ha!

How do we know that Rome was built in a night?

History tells us it wasn't built in a day.

How does Moses make tea?

Hebrews it.

Haaaa!

Why did Henry VIII have so many wives?

He liked to chop and change.

Who was the most reasonable pharaoh in Egypt?

Pharaoh Nuff.

Ha!

What happened to Lady Godiva's horse when he found out she wasn't wearing any clothes?

It made him shy.

LOL!

What did the damsel in distress say to the knight?

"Don't just sit there. Slay something."

John: "I wish I had been alive a few hundred years ago."

Teacher: "Why?"

John: "There would have been a lot less history to learn."

LOL!

Who invented fire?

Some bright spark.

Why did the mummy have a holiday?

He wanted to unwind.

Ha!

Why does history keep repeating itself?

Nobody was listening the first time.

What did the dragon say when he met a knight in shining armour?

"I love tinned food."

Caesar: "What's the weather like?"

Brutus: "Hail, Caesar."

LOL!

Why were the early days of history called the Dark Ages?

There were lots of knights.

Why did knights in armour practise a lot?

To stop them getting rusty.

How do mummies begin their emails?

Tomb it may concern.

LOL!

When a knight was killed in battle, what sign did they put on his grave?

Rust in peace.

LOL!

Haaaa!

Why is England the wettest country?

Because the queen has reigned there for years.

Where was the Declaration of Independence signed?

At the bottom.

What kind of lighting did Noah use for the ark?

Floodlights.

How was the Roman Empire divided?

With a pair of Caesars.

Who built the ark?

I have Noah idea.

SILLINESS AT SCHOOL

You spend a lot of time at school and it's the perfect place to tell some great jokes. Make your friends roll around with laughter at these brilliant puns and one-liners.

Ha! Hee Heeee!

What do you call a dog that's also a librarian?

A hush puppy.

Why did the music teacher need a ladder?

So she could reach the high notes.

LOL!

Why was the nose sad after the audition?

He didn't get picked.

What are the longest tables in the world?

Multiplication tables.

LOL!

Haaaa!

What do you call a teacher wearing headphones?

Anything you like. He can't hear you.

When can school uniforms be fire hazards?

When they are blazers.

Which subject do snakes like to learn?

Hiss-tory.

HAAAA!

Why did the baseball player take his bat to the library?

Because his teacher told him to hit the books.

Ha! Hee Heeee!

Why did the science teacher jump in the lake?

He wanted to test the water.

Why was the algebra book sad?

Because it had too many problems.

LOL!

Teacher: "Why is your exam paper blank?"

Kyle: "I used invisible ink."

Which type of snake is good at sums?

An adder.

Ha!

How do you make the number one vanish?

Put a 'G' at the start and it's gone.

LOL!

Teacher: "Why didn't you do your homework, you lazy boy?"

Chris: "You can't tell me off for something I didn't do."

What did the bookworm say to the school librarian?

"Please can I burrow this book?"

Haaaa!

What happened to the plant in the classroom?

It grew square roots.

LOL!

Why are fish really smart?

Because they live in schools.

What did the ruler say to the pencil?

"You're looking pretty sharp today."

Why was the teacher so good at teaching geography?

He had abroad knowledge of his subject.

Haaaa!

LOL!

What did the page say to the cover?

"You're squishing me."

Kath: "My teacher doesn't know anything."

Lee: "Why do you think that?"

Kath: "All she does is ask questions."

How did the geography student drown?

His grades were below C-level.

What did the pen say to the paper?

"Are you sure that's the write answer?"

Teacher: "What do you get if you multiply 5689 by 20?"

Eva: "The wrong answer."

What do you call a rock that doesn't show up for school?

A skipping stone.

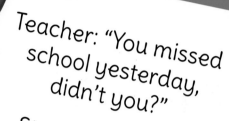

Teacher: "You missed school yesterday, didn't you?"

Student: "No, not very much."

Ha!

Why did the teacher wear dark glasses?

Because the class was so bright.

Why did the student throw his watch out of the classroom window?

He wanted to see time fly.

KNOCK-KNOCK SILLINESS

You know how they work. Find the ones you like the most and impress your friends with these super-silly KNOCK-KNOCK jokes.

KNOCK-KNOCK.

Who's there?

Hatch.

Hatch who?

Bless you.

LOL!

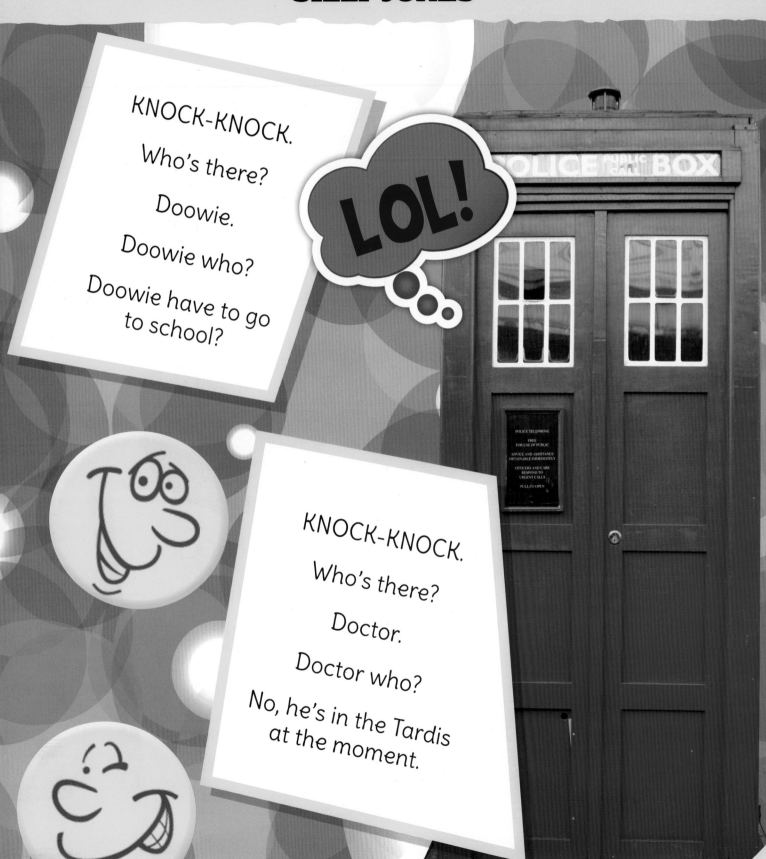

KNOCK-KNOCK.

Who's there?

Doowie.

Doowie who?

Doowie have to go to school?

LOL!

KNOCK-KNOCK.

Who's there?

Doctor.

Doctor who?

No, he's in the Tardis at the moment.

POLICE CALL BOX

POLICE TELEPHONE
FREE
FOR USE OF PUBLIC
ADVICE AND ASSISTANCE
OBTAINABLE IMMEDIATELY
OFFICERS AND CARS
RESPOND TO
URGENT CALLS
PULL TO OPEN

KNOCK-KNOCK.

Who's there?

Harry.

Harry who?

Harry up and open this door.

KNOCK-KNOCK.

Who's there?

Isabel.

Isabel who?

Isabel necessary on a bicycle?

KNOCK-KNOCK.

Who's there?

Banana.

Banana who?

KNOCK-KNOCK.

Who's there?

Banana.

Banana who?

KNOCK-KNOCK.

Who's there?

Banana.

Banana who?

KNOCK-KNOCK.

Who's there?

Orange.

Orange who?

Orange you glad I didn't say banana?

LOL!

KNOCK-KNOCK.

Who's there?

Cows go.

Cows go who?

No, cows go moo.

KNOCK-KNOCK.

Who's there?

Arthur.

Arthur who?

Arthur got.

KNOCK-KNOCK.

Who's there?

Roach.

Roach who?

Roach you a letter.
Did you get it?

Ha!

KNOCK-KNOCK.

Who's there?

A herd.

A herd who?

A herd you were home, so I came over.

KNOCK-KNOCK.

Who's there?

Adore.

Adore who?

Adore is between us. Open up.

Haaaa!

KNOCK-KNOCK.

Who's there?

Ben.

Ben who?

Ben knocking for ten minutes now.

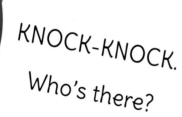

KNOCK-KNOCK.

Who's there?

Lettuce.

Lettuce who?

Lettuce in.
It's cold out here.

Ha!

Haaaa!

KNOCK-KNOCK.

Who's there?

Canoe.

Canoe who?

Canoe help me with my homework?

KNOCK-KNOCK.

Who's there?

Woo.

Woo who?

Woo-hoo to you, too.

LATERS, TATERS

Ha!

LOL!